THIS
JOURNAL
OF
TRANSFORMING
ENCOUNTERS
BELONGS
TO:

The Spirit Moves: 30 Transforming Encounters

Visit our Web site: **www.grouppublishing.com**

Credits:
Contributing Writers: Jenny Baker, Rick Beno, Debbie Gowensmith, Mikal Keefer,
    Joy-Elizabeth Lawrence, James W. Miller, and Christina Schofield
Editor: Kelli B. Trujillo
Creative Development Editor: Amy Simpson
Chief Creative Officer: Joani Schultz
Assistant Editor: Alison Imbriaco
Art Director: Jean Bruns
Cover & Interior Design: Liz Howe Design [LizHoweDesign.com], with special thanks to
    James Dietz, Michael Emanuele, and Valerie Romero
Production Manager: Dodie Tipton

Library of Congress Cataloging-in-Publication Data
The Spirit moves : 30 transforming encounters.
      p. cm.
   ISBN 0-7644-2418-1 (hardcover : alk. paper)
      1. Holy Spirit—Meditations. I. Group Publishing.
   BT121.3 .S65 2002
   242—dc21   2002001830

Printed in China.
10 9 8 7 6 5 4 3 2 1   01 00 09 08 07 06 05 04 03 02

The Spirit...moves.

God's presence in this world. God's presence in your soul. The Holy Spirit—
moving in our planet...and in *your* life. Empowering you.
Comforting you. Guiding you. Drawing you ever closer into God's
mysterious presence and overwhelming love.

This journal of thirty personal devotions will transform your understanding
of the role the Spirit plays in your life. You'll learn to surrender to
the Spirit's leading...to listen to the Spirit's words...to keep in step
with the Spirit's guidance. You'll explore new depths in your personal
encounters with God. Everyday things that once seemed routine and
ordinary will become extraordinary. You'll sense and experience
God's presence in your life like never before.

Each of these devotions will prompt you to *do* or *experience* something,
will encourage you to meditate on Scripture, will give you thoughts
and ideas to consider. And you can journal your thoughts, your questions,
your prayers—just between you and God.

Do one devotion each day for thirty days, or spread the devotions out over a
longer time frame. Use this journal for your own personal time with
God or use it with a group of friends.

Open your spiritual eyes. Quiet your soul.

Prepare to experience the powerful presence of God's spirit...moving.

Poor Reception

The Spirit...moves.

Listen to a radio in your room. Turn the dial until you hear
nothing but static.

Listen carefully. Can you hear any words or music?
Can you decipher anything?

Almost—but not quite.

There's a radio station broadcasting on the frequency you've selected,
but the transmitter isn't close enough. There's a station somewhere
trying to connect with you. Trying to bring you the talk, music, news,
and commercials its staff has created and sent out onto the airwaves.

You're just not close enough to hear it.

Now dial in a station that plays gentle, quiet music clearly.

Hear it? The signal is crisp and clear and, most important,
close enough that you can receive it.

God is not far away. He's near. God has set up camp in your
neighborhood. Your room. Your life.

If you've committed your life to him, you can believe he's there
in the person of the Holy Spirit. It's a promise.

Read Acts 2:37-39 aloud.

Read it again, slowly.

This promise isn't just for those who stood, brokenhearted,
in an audience that could hear Peter's words.

The promise is for you, too.

Are you listening?

Pray.

WHOM the LORD

*Thoughts,
feelings,
musings,
dreams,
pictures,
ideas...*

Our GOD WILL CALL

Significance

The Spirit. . .moves.

Some days it's easy to feel insignificant
in this huge, busy world. Everyone
wears similar clothing from similar stores;
everyone eats fast food; everyone hears
the same songs on the radio; everyone sees
the same billboards that start the cycle all over again.
You may even share the same name with people at school or work.

Read Job 33:3-6. As Elihu begins his speech to Job, he includes a vital
element for all believers in God—that we were created
and given life by God.

Close your eyes and imagine the breath of the Almighty giving you life.
Does it look like CPR? Does it feel like a whisper? Think about all
the intricacies of your body—cell reproduction,
your immune system, the color bursts in your eyes.

Take an ink pad or a marker and make some thumb or
fingerprints on the next page. Follow the swirls and dips
in the maze—completely unique to you.
No one else's fingerprints will match yours.

Elihu said, "I am just like you before God," speaking about
the sinful nature of mankind. We are all sinful,
yet God has made our fingerprints, irises, and
DNA different from everyone else's.

Thank God for the uniquenesses he has given you. Thank him for giving
you the breath of life and significance, even in a crazy, bustling
world. Ask him to help you remember to look at your hands—
your fingerprints—when you start to forget how you were made.

Pray.

THE SPIRIT OF GOD HAS MADE ME

HOW GOD MET ME

*Thoughts,
feelings,
musings,
dreams,
pictures,
ideas...*

THE BREATH OF THE ALMIGHTY GIVES ME LIFE.

Poured Out

The Spirit...moves.

What's your favorite song—one that makes you feel good? Energizes you?

Spend some time all alone listening to your favorite song. If possible, use headphones so you can play your song as loudly as you want! Make sure you can't hear anything else.

How do you feel? What kinds of words do you hear? What kinds of messages? What does the song move you to do?

Listen to the song again and do something it moves you to do. Jump, sway, dance, kick, spin, sing along.

Read Romans 5:5.

Listening to music is like pouring a song into your head; the Holy Spirit pours love into your heart. Through the Holy Spirit's power, you can see beyond faults and despite selfishness and without prejudices and past your own fear. You can see someone the way God sees that person. And then, through the same power, you can love that person.

How can you listen to God as intently as you listened to your favorite song? How can you shut out all distractions? How can you open yourself to have God's love poured out into your heart?

Talk to God. Focus on what God says to you through the Holy Spirit more than on what you want to ask from God.

What is the Spirit telling you? How is the Spirit moving you?

Act upon it.

Pray.

HOW GOD MET ME

Thoughts,
feelings,
musings,
dreams,
pictures,
ideas...

Wheels

The Spirit . . . moves.

Go for a walk along your street or in a park.

See how far you can get in three minutes.

As you walk, breathe deeply. Think about the muscles you're using.

Now, go back to your starting place and travel that same distance again,
    but this time on wheels—a skateboard,
    Rollerblades, a bike, or a scooter.

How quickly can you travel the distance that took three minutes to walk?

See how fast you can go. Enjoy the sensation of speed,
    the wind on your face, your ability to glide.

The muscles you used when you walked are still working hard,
    but it's fun because the wheels add so much to your speed.

Read Acts 1:4-8.

The Spirit anoints what we do, touching our lives with his power,
    putting wheels under our feet. Not pushing us along while we do
    nothing, but adding his energy to our effort to enable us to glide.

Think about your journey through life.

Where do you struggle? Where does it feel like you are trudging along,
    one step after the other, without making much progress?
    Where have you given up because you seemed to be getting nowhere?

Ask the Spirit to anoint those areas, to touch them with his
    life and power.

Ask him to put wheels under your feet.

And then start moving.

Pray.

you will be
BAPTIZED

HOW GOD MET ME

Thoughts,
feelings,
musings,
dreams,
pictures,
ideas...

WITH THE HOLY SPIRIT

Higher Ways

The Spirit. . .moves.

Quantification. Hydroxylamine. Croustade. Flip through the pages of a dictionary, and look for words you've never heard of before. Think for a minute about all that you don't know.

Surely you have had that sinking feeling—as you crammed for a geometry test or looked through a new computer program. It comes when you learn just enough to realize how much you don't know.

When you were a child, your world was limited. There were probably times when you felt independent or thought you could make better decisions than your parents. They might have been amused as you stubbornly learned lessons the hard way.

Read Romans 11:33-36.

Consider how very little we actually understand about God's higher ways. It's ironic that realizing how little we know might be our first glimmer of wisdom!

Imagine how silly you would feel telling a rocket scientist how to operate a telephone. Or how ridiculous it would be to offer Albert Einstein advice about arithmetic. These verses remind us that God knows all and doesn't need us to explain to him what is best. He can be trusted.

The Holy Spirit is a mystery. As long as we live on earth, we will probably never understand these higher ways— how the Spirit helps us when we pray, guides us in decisions, and protects us from harm. The Holy Spirit is sometimes referred to as the "Comforter." Perhaps the greatest "comfort" of all is realizing we don't have to *know* everything.

Pray.

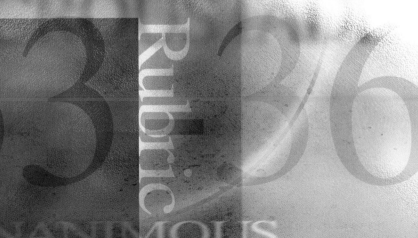

VISCERAL

fication

quiddity

lagrant

Rubric

3 36

NANIMOUS

*Thoughts,
feelings,
musings,
Dreams,
pictures,
ideas...*

Speech

The Spirit . . . moves.

Do you like spicy foods? Even if you don't, fix yourself a snack that includes something spicy. Try chips and hot salsa, jalapeño poppers (from the freezer section at the grocery store), spicy Indian curry (from your favorite Indian restaurant), or a sandwich or pizza with hot peppers.

Enjoy.

Now how does your mouth feel? How do you react when you eat something spicy?

Maybe you gulp a glass of water. Maybe you fan your mouth with your hand. Maybe you take short, shallow breaths. Maybe you close your mouth, relish the burn, and start to sweat.

Whatever you do, it's practically automatic. Your body sends a signal to your brain that says, "Help!" Your brain reacts, sending signals to your body. Before you know it, you're gulping a glass of water. Your mouth feels better.

What other automatic reactions do you have? How do you know what to do?

Read Mark 13:11.

Did you know the Holy Spirit has the power to give you words to say? Not words to crush or intimidate, but words to teach and to reveal God's Spirit.

The Holy Spirit knows what to say, even when *you* don't. And just as your brain moves you to cool down your spice-abused mouth, the Holy Spirit moves you to speak.

Have you ever spoken God's words?

If you don't remember that a glass of water is available when your mouth is burning, your brain will find an alternative. Likewise, if you don't rely on the Holy Spirit within you for words to say, you'll find an alternative to God's words—your own.

How can you learn to be available to speak what the Holy Spirit knows to say?

Think about the kinds of words God wants you to use in his name.

Pray.

FOR IT IS NOT YOU SPEAKING, BUT THE HOLY SPIRIT

HOW GOD MET ME

*Thoughts,
feelings,
musings,
dreams,
pictures,
ideas...*

you

not you

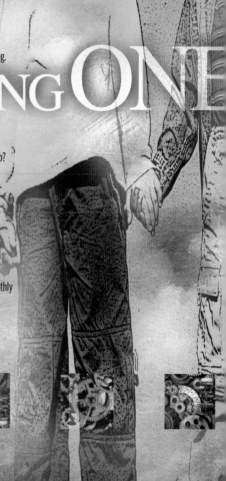

Running Smoothly

The Spirit…moves.

Prop a car hood open and look at the engine while it's running.
    Listen to the hum, and watch
    (don't touch!) all the many parts
    that make the car go.

What smell does the engine give off?
    How might it smell if one of the parts was out of place?
    Not cooperating? Causing friction? Overheating?

What would happen if just one of the parts failed to do its job?

Imagine being in a car that stalls on the road. We may not
    notice the importance of cooperation until it fails.

The same is true in relationships. Your relationships with
    others can run smoothly…and they can stall.
    In what ways do your relationships with other people
    function like the engine? When do they not?

Read Philippians 2:1-2.

God wants us to be united with the Spirit and one another.
    When Christians listen to the Spirit, we can be like a smoothly
    running engine. But when we put ourselves before others,
    when we're out of step with the Spirit,
    we're like an engine with parts that won't cooperate…
    and there is friction…and overheating.

What can make your relationships run like the engine?
    What would smoothly running relationships
    look like for you? What is the Spirit calling
    you to do in your relationships?

Give thanks for the Spirit's work in building
    unity between believers.

Pray.

BEING ONE

INSPIRIT

Thoughts,
feelings,
musings,
dreams,
pictures,
ideas...

Balloon

The Spirit. . .moves.

Find a balloon, one that hasn't been blown up yet, and sit with it
in the palm of your hand. What can it do, this flat,
disappointing piece of lifeless rubber? Throw it up and catch it;
squeeze it and pull it. Is this really something
that kids love to play with?

Then add the magic ingredient. Lift it to your lips and gently breathe
your life into this balloon. Feel it expand under your fingers.
Keep blowing until it is fat and round. Tie a knot in it and
pat it around the room. Hit it up and watch it gently float down.
Tie some string onto the balloon.

Now go outside into the wind. Hold the string and let the balloon
be pushed around by the wind.
(If it's not very windy, you may need to imagine this!)

And then let it go. Allow the wind to take the balloon where it wants.
Watch the balloon fly, bounce, float, and fall.
Imagine its journey to new places, new possibilities.

Read Genesis 2:7.

God breathed life into dust and created a person. Throughout history,
God has continued to breathe his life into his people,
awakening, creating, restoring.

But those who receive the breath of God need to be ready to
go where the Spirit takes them. Are you ready to be
like the balloon that has no control of its own
direction? Are you ready to let go?

Stand tall, stretch your arms wide, breathe deeply,
and surrender to the Spirit.

God knows where you'll end up.

Pray.

the breath

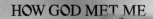

*Thoughts,
feelings,
musings,
dreams,
pictures,
ideas...*

of life

The Playground

The Spirit...moves.

Find an empty children's playground in a public
    park and stand outside it.

Think about the games you played when
    you were a child.

What rules governed your games?

The rules of the games determined who won...
    who was out of bounds. Why do children
    call upon the rules to decide what is fair?

Who decided what the rules were?

Your daily activities have changed since childhood.
    Do rules still guide you in the same way?

Think about the boundaries God has set for you.
    How do they protect you? How might they
    limit you? Who decides what the rules say?

The Holy Spirit serves as an internal rule book and
    teacher, reminding you of the rules and
    inclining your heart to follow.

Read Galatians 4:1-7.

God gave us laws to help us learn how to live,
    like children learning to play fair.
    But at the right time, God sent the Spirit of his Son
    into our hearts to be our guide, to fulfill the laws.

Thank God for raising you as a beloved child.
    Thank God for sending the Spirit into your heart
    to be your guide.

How will you listen to the call of the Spirit
    in order to follow God?

Pray.

BECAUSE

HOW GOD MET ME

Thoughts,
feelings,
musings,
dreams,
pictures,
ideas...

YOU ARE

Out With the Old

The Spirit...moves.

Do you like to clean out your closet, desk, or files? When you were a child, were you ever encouraged to get rid of old toys—to sell them, give them away, or throw them out? Do you ever dispose of something old in order to buy something new?

Think about your stuff. What can you throw out or give away? Old shoes? A shirt you've had for six years? Sunglasses you don't wear any more? Look through your closet and drawers and get rid of something—or several things.

What you own tells something about who you are— it shows your taste in colors, what sports you like to participate in, who gives you Christmas or birthday presents. Often, when something says nothing about a person, it's discarded.

Read Ezekiel 11:18-21.

Here God explains how he will clean out the souls of his people. He will throw out their stone heart and implant a heart of flesh and a new spirit.

Ponder your spirit. What does it say about you?

Do you follow God's decrees?

Are you devoted to God?

Do you need God to give you a spirit transplant like the transplant he wanted to give the Israelites?

Expose your spirit to God. Let him work within you.

Pray.

detestable id
an undivided heart
spirit in them; I will
them their heart of
them a heart of flesh,
follow my decrees and
keep my law The
e, and I w be
those
to

Thoughts,
feelings,
musings,
dreams,
pictures,
ideas...

spirit

done,
n Lord,

e Iron

Spirit…moves.

e a piece of your clothing on an ironing board.
Plug in an iron and let it warm.
prepare for a challenge: Start ironing.
ly too much heat and you'll scorch the clothing.
Slide the iron too gently across the fabric and
you won't accomplish anything.
ing calls for a delicate balance. You use heat and
pressure to shape your clothing, to smooth imperfections,
to get your shirt or slacks crisp and looking their best.
way, heat and pressure combine to mold you, too…
and shape you…and prompt you to deliver your best.
To become your best.
To do what you thought was beyond you.
a delicate process, and you probably resent every minute of it.
don't enjoy being molded. We'd rather avoid pain.
And it may feel unfair that God uses pressure
and heat to call us closer to him—
the pressures of a world in need to prompt our
response, the heat of our passions to ignite a
love for him and his purposes.
d the promise in I Corinthians 10:12-13, and let the
words sink deep into your soul.
ssure and heat aren't your enemies. You needn't fear
them. The pressure will never be too great,
the heat never overwhelming.
ause you're not alone in the pressure cooker.
The Holy Spirit walks with you.
y.

SO,
IF YOU THINK
YOU ARE
STANDING
FIRM, *be careful*

*Thoughts,
feelings,
musings,
dreams,
pictures,
ideas...*

that you don't fall!

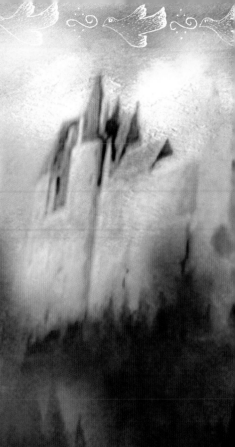

A Heavenly Home

The Spirit...moves.

Think of the most luxurious home you've seen in
real life—a mansion, a castle, or a beautiful farm.
What about it appeals to you? How much do people
pay for homes like that? How hard do they work?
How long do they save? Why?

Now borrow a tent from someone you know and find
a place to set it up, outdoors or inside.

How much would people pay to live in that tent for
the rest of their lives? How hard would they
work *not* to?

Lie down inside it. How different would it feel to
wake up in a tent rather than in a mansion?
What would you notice first in the morning?

Compare the world you live in now to heaven.
How are they different? What would it be like to
wake up in heaven rather than on earth?
What would you notice first?

Read 2 Corinthians 5:1-5.

The earth is like a tent compared to the mansion
of heaven. All you need is a key to get in.
The Spirit is the key, the proof that you belong
there—your reservation for heaven.

How can you live as if you belong to a heavenly home?
Pray.

WE HAVE A BU

Thoughts, feelings, musings, dreams, pictures, ideas...

an eternal house in heaven

LDING FROM GOD

Protection

The Spirit. . .moves.

What's the cost of protection?

For a country, it may be billions of dollars.
    For your car, a coat of wax may handle it.

For the place you live, it's probably rows of
    overlapping shingles that deflect the rain and
    shrug off the snow.

Take a few moments now to go to your garage or attic.
    Someplace where you can look up and see the
    underside of your shingled roof.

Shingles protect everything beneath them,
    but look at the plywood they're attached to.
    Nails used to fasten down the shingles puncture
    and splinter the wood.

Are the shingles doing their job of protecting the wood?
    Yes—but at a cost.

Protection is never free. It always costs something.

If you love and follow God, he's with you.
    He dwells in you in the person of the Holy Spirit.

But that protection comes at a cost.

Read I Corinthians 6:19-20.

You are protected.

What's the cost?

Pray.

Thoughts,
feelings,
musings,
dreams,
pictures,
ideas...

Sight

The Spirit...moves.

If you wear glasses, take them off.
> (If you don't wear glasses, put on some dark
> sunglasses and wear them inside your home.)

Look up a number in the phone book. Fix yourself a snack.
> Check the clock—what time is it?
> Surf the 'Net. Look out a window.

What do you see? What *don't* you see that you wish you could?

What's it like to be without something you really need? What other
> needs do you have? What could you just not live without?

Trying to figure out how to get along without something you need
> can be frustrating. Uncomfortable. Even frightening.

Read Psalm 51:10-12.

Why was the Holy Spirit important to David?

How do you think David felt about the pestering thought
> that he might have to get along without the Holy Spirit?

What about you? What's it like when you feel you're without God?
> When God feels far away and it's been awhile since you've connected?

It's a desperate feeling. We need God's Spirit to guide us,
> to comfort us, to restore us, to cleanse us. Just the idea—
> even a fleeting thought—that God's Spirit might not be
> with us leaves us lost and vulnerable. Even frightened.

Christ promised that the Holy Spirit would always be with us.
> God doesn't take the Holy Spirit from us. God restores us. Purifies us.
> God's Spirit is always with us.

How does it feel to know that God's Spirit—God's very presence—
> is always with you?

Reflect on David's words in Psalm 51:10-12 one more time.

Pray.

Thoughts,
feelings,
musings,
dreams,
pictures,
ideas...

from your present

If you can, go outside and gather some dry sticks. Pile them together in your fireplace, a grill, or an old coffee can. Light them to make a small fire.

If you can't build a fire, stay indoors and light a candle.

Watch the flame dance and flicker, clinging to the sticks or the wick.

A fire needs fuel, oxygen, and heat to burn.

Have you ever helped to build a big bonfire?

Think back to that time (or imagine it).

Picture logs of wood being thrown onto the fire.

    Hear the crackling as the flames take hold.

    Watch the sparks fly into the night sky.

    What would you need to do to put this fire out?

Feel the warmth from your own small flame in front of you.

Read 1 Thessalonians 5:16-22.

Do not put out the Spirit's fire.

At Pentecost, the disciples saw the Spirit as tongues of fire that rested on each of them.

The Spirit burns in you, warming your heart with God's presence. Think about what keeps this flame bright.

    What is the spark that sets your heart alight?

    What is the fuel that feeds the fire of the Spirit?

    What fans the flames into life?

Will you tend the fire? Or let it go out?

Be joyful always; pray continually;

    give thanks at all times. . .

    and the Spirit will burn in you.

Watch your flame flicker and dance, a reflection of the Spirit within you.

Thoughts,
feelings,
musings,
Dreams,
pictures,
Ideas...

JOYFUL

YFUL

Branded

The Spirit. . .moves.

Open your closet. Take out a piece of clothing that has
a logo stitched on it. Put on the T-shirt, jeans,
shoes, or hat—whatever it is you're holding.

Now look at yourself in the mirror for a long moment.

What does this logo say about you? About the company,
band, or sports team the logo represents?
What image does the logo communicate?
What feeling is the logo supposed to prompt in you?

Does it work? Do you think that way, feel that way,
act that way?

And what do others assume about you when they
see you wearing the logo?

Now pretend that you want to pull on a logo that
communicates to others that you're a
Christ-follower—that you know Jesus.

What logo would you pick?

Lots of logos have been tried. Carrying a Bible.
Message T-shirts. Praying before lunch in the
cafeteria. A cross necklace.

But in the end they're just logos—they're external.
God has provided another way for others to
see that you're one of his.
And it's not about how you look—
it's about how you live.

Read Ephesians 1:13.

You've been branded. How will that look today?

Pray.

Thoughts,
feelings,
musings,
dreams,
pictures,
ideas...

aving believed, you were marked in him with a seal

MISED HOLY SPIRIT

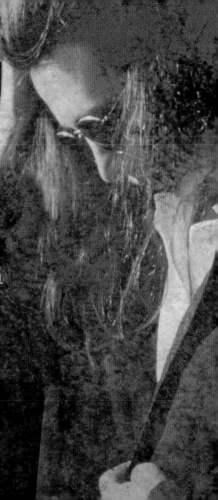

No Hiding

The Spirit...moves.

Remember playing Hide-and-Seek when you were growing up?

Look around you. Where is the best place to hide?

Could you hide from someone where you are right now?

Go to the best hiding place and hide yourself.

Would someone walking by see you?

Think about how good your hiding place is.

Would it keep you secret?

As we get older, we don't play Hide-and-Seek anymore.

But we still like to hide. Sometimes we hide our true thoughts from others. Sometimes we hide from ourselves. Sometimes we try to hide from God.

Read Psalm 139:7-10.

You can try to hide from God's Spirit...

but God sees everything you do.

God knows everything you think. God knows everything you feel.

Scary thoughts? Maybe, but comforting ones too.

You're never alone. You're never without someone who understands you. You're never abandoned.

Never.

God lives in you. His Spirit knows you. Guides you. Holds you.

You may be trying to hide from God's Spirit.

But where will you go?

Why hide from someone who cares for you so much?

Pray.

Ask God's Spirit to hold you close to him.

And if you have been hiding...ask to be found.

*Thoughts,
feelings,
musings,
dreams,
pictures,
ideas...*

YOUR
RIGHT
HAND
will hold me fast

Spiritual Portraits

The Spirit...moves.

Draw a picture of yourself. Take time to observe your face in
    a mirror and capture the details on paper.

    What things do you like about the way you look?

    What things would you like to change?

    Can you see traces of your parents in your appearance?

Imagine what your spiritual portrait looks like to God.

    When he looks deep inside you, what does he find there?

    What are your best features?

    What parts of you would God like to remodel?

Can he find traces of himself inside you? Can he see his
    resemblance as you tell your friends that you belong to him?

The Holy Spirit living inside you is like the spiritual DNA that shows
    you are God's child. Others can see the resemblance at a glance.

Read Philippians 1:6.

God will never just quit or give up on you.

    The Holy Spirit is always at work making your insides
    more beautiful. You can be sure that, as you grow
    spiritually, you will look more and more like your Father.

As you make daily decisions about what to do and say,
    think of the effect each motive and action
    has on your spiritual portrait.

    Are the choices you are making improving
    your spiritual appearance?

    Work alongside the Holy Spirit
    to grow in character.

    Your insides will be lookin' good!

Pray.

Skill

The Spirit . . . moves.

Find something within your house that's handcrafted.

Maybe it's an antique bureau, a piece of pottery, needle-point or
cross-stitched work, homemade napkins, or a rocking chair.

What caused this item to be made? Need or necessity? Desire to create?

Materials to create with?

Touch this item—examine the details, feel the texture—is it a rough textile or smooth,
sanded wood? What was it originally?

Was it a mineral deep in the earth?

Was it a tree in the center of the forest?

Was it harvested from a plant in the hot, dry regions of the South?

Read Exodus 31:1-11.

Think about what God said about Bezalel:

"I have filled him with the Spirit of God, with skill,
ability and knowledge in all kinds of crafts."

The Spirit fills us all with gifts.

Think about the handcrafted items in your house.

Are any of them things you made?

Were they made for someone or something special, just as Bezalel
formed the components of the Tabernacle for God?

What can you make?

What does your skill, ability, and knowledge enable you to do?

Does it glorify God?

Thank God for the abilities he has given you.

Ask him if there is more he wants you to learn.

Consider making something that will bring glory to God and his creation.

Pray.

HOW GOD MET ME

*Thoughts,
feelings,
musings,
dreams,
pictures,
ideas...*

*I have given skill
to all the craftsmen
to make anything
I have
commanded you.*

Applause

The Spirit...moves.

Turn on your television to a sporting event. Observe the cheering crowd. Watch the faces as fans support their team. Why are they so spirited? so passionate? As they root for their team, they seem like a part of the game— consumed by what is playing out before them. Cheer along. Applaud!

Now, close your eyes and imagine the applause is not for a player or team, but for God.

Read Revelation 4:8-11.

In Revelation, the Bible paints a picture of heaven. Enormous crowds, all of creation, are cheering God on. People from every nation and era join heavenly beings in praise of their Maker.

Try to picture that scene. Next time you are in a large, cheering crowd, close your eyes and remember these verses. Imagine you are there before God, applauding.

The Holy Spirit plays an important part in worship. He moves inside of us, reminding us that God is present and is good. He urges us to worship. He translates our prayers and worship to God.

When you feel the Spirit move, worship.

Pray.

HOW GOD MET ME

Thoughts,
feelings,
musings,
dreams,
pictures,
ideas...

holy, holy, holy

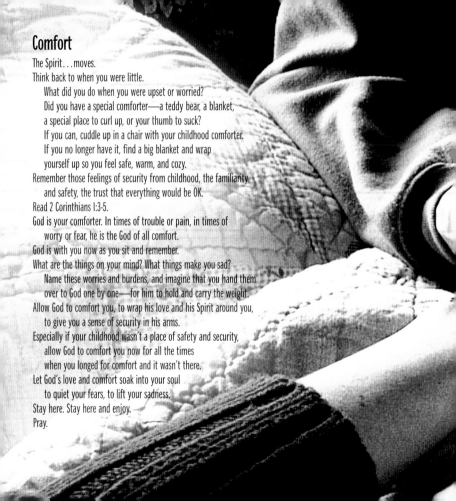

Comfort

The Spirit...moves.

Think back to when you were little.

What did you do when you were upset or worried?
Did you have a special comforter—a teddy bear, a blanket,
a special place to curl up, or your thumb to suck?
If you can, cuddle up in a chair with your childhood comforter.
If you no longer have it, find a big blanket and wrap
yourself up so you feel safe, warm, and cozy.

Remember those feelings of security from childhood, the familiarity
and safety, the trust that everything would be OK.

Read 2 Corinthians 1:3-5.

God is your comforter. In times of trouble or pain, in times of
worry or fear, he is the God of all comfort.

God is with you now as you sit and remember.

What are the things on your mind? What things make you sad?
Name these worries and burdens, and imagine that you hand them
over to God one by one—for him to hold and carry the weight.

Allow God to comfort you, to wrap his love and his Spirit around you,
to give you a sense of security in his arms.

Especially if your childhood wasn't a place of safety and security,
allow God to comfort you now for all the times
when you longed for comfort and it wasn't there.

Let God's love and comfort soak into your soul
to quiet your fears, to lift your sadness.

Stay here. Stay here and enjoy.

Pray.

Thoughts, feelings, musings, dreams, pictures, ideas...

Our comfort overflows

Have Hope

The Spirit...moves.

Find a comfortable, quiet place where you can sit and think.

Take an egg with you.

As you sit, turn the egg gently in your hands. Feel the
   smoothness. Explore the egg with your fingertips.
   Feel the imperfections, the slight roughness.

Continue to explore the texture of the egg, carefully.
   To you, an egg may represent nothing more than breakfast.
   But in some other cultures, it represents far more:
   the hope for new life, the hope of a future.

Think about your future for a few moments.
   How do you feel about your future?
   Are you hopeful?
   Hopeless?
   Or somewhere in between?

How do you feel about your future when you consider your circumstances?
   Your plans?

The egg you hold is fragile, but full of promise. Given the right circumstances,
   an egg's thin shell can protect a heartbeat.

Your future may feel equally fragile—one wrong move and
   you'll crack open or be tossed aside.

But you needn't be fearful.

Read Romans 15:13.

You're held in the hands of someone who knows you and knows your future.
   Someone who loves you. Someone who wants you to experience peace, joy, and hope.

Bask in God's love today.

Pray.

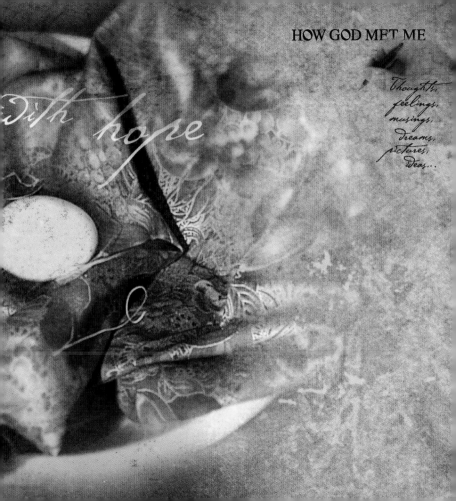

HOW GOD MET ME

Thoughts,
feelings,
musings,
dreams,
pictures,
ideas...

with hope

Filled

The Spirit . . . moves.

Find a teapot and some jagged stones or a bunch of grapes.

Stand the teapot in the kitchen sink and fill it with the stones or grapes.

 Fill it to the brim, until you can't squeeze in any more.

The teapot is full—but it's *not* full.

If you peer inside, you can see spaces, little pockets of emptiness.

If you had smaller stones you could maybe drop them in,

 but the teapot can never be completely full of jagged stones—

 there'd still be tiny gaps hidden away.

Now empty the teapot and stand it in the sink again. This time fill it with water.

 Watch the water level rise as the liquid spreads to fill every part of the teapot.

Read Ephesians 3:14-19.

This is how God wants to fill you with his Spirit—slowly and persistently

 pouring his love and his life into every part of who you are,

 missing nothing, avoiding nothing, touching everything.

Invite the Spirit into every part of your life so you are "filled to the measure

 of all the fullness of God." Close your eyes and breathe deeply as you picture

 the Spirit filling you. Pause . . . and enjoy God.

But that's not all. Add a little more water to your teapot and watch it overflow.

 Ask God for more of his Spirit so that you overflow with his love.

 Who do you want to pass it on to?

Pray.

all the fullness of God

Thoughts,
feelings,
musings,
dreams,
pictures,
ideas...

Same Spirit

The Spirit...moves.

Do you remember being in preschool or kindergarten and talking
about sharing? Do you remember sharing with your
friends or siblings? Was it difficult to share
favorite toys with "unfavorite" people?
Do you sometimes struggle with sharing now?

It's hard to share things when you're afraid that someone else
will scratch your CDs, tear your book, rip or dirty your clothes.
It's easy to be selfish.

As Christians, we're commanded to give to people in need.
We're also told that we all share the same Spirit.

Read 1 Corinthians 12:12-13.

"I'm my own person!" a lot of people say. But here we read that
we're all one body, that we are all given the one Spirit to drink.

While God made each of us unique, he designed us to be our best
when we work with the whole of his people—
as part of the body.

How can you share yourself in the midst of the body of Christ?

How can you drink the Spirit with others?

Think about this while you prepare a drink
to share with another person.
Stir up some lemonade, make some tea,
or brew some coffee.
Invite someone to partake with you.
Serve that person.
Talk about how we are all
given the same Spirit.

Thank God for this.

Pray.

slave
or
free...

*Thoughts,
feelings,
musings,
dreams,
pictures,
ideas...*

*one
Spirit
to drink*

Seed

The Spirit…moves.

Find a seed, then go to a garden or park where there's soil or
   dirt you can dig through. (If you can't find a seed, buy some
   seeds or use a seed from an apple or orange you've cut open.)

Hold the seed in the palm of your hand.

Do you know what potential is locked away inside this seed?
   Picture it in your mind as a fully grown plant.
   (If you don't know what type of plant the seed came from,
   let your imagination run wild!)

But what will happen to the seed if it stays in the palm of your hand?

What does it need in order to grow? Earth, water, food, and light.

Make a small hole in the dirt.
   Put the seed in it and cover it with soil.
   Give it some water.

In time the seed will push roots down into the soil
   and send a shoot upward to find the light.
   It will stretch and grow.
   All the secret potential hidden inside it will be seen and enjoyed.

Read Galatians 6:7-9.

What are you sowing in your life?

How many of the things you say and do will grow and bear fruit for God?

How many of your thoughts and attitudes will blossom like
   beautiful flowers…and fill the air with the scent of the Spirit?

Probably not all of them——but don't be discouraged.

Do good; pursue truth; love holiness.

Let the Spirit feed and nurture your heart.

And in time you *will* reap a harvest.

Pray.

Thoughts,
feelings,
musings,
dreams,
pictures,
ideas...

VESP

at the proper time

Vision

Even on my servants

The Spirit...moves.

Take some binoculars or a telescope outside.
 (If you don't have binoculars or a telescope,
 you can look the wrong way through a camera
 view window.) Find a place high up, on a hill or a tall
 building, where you can stand and look into the distance.

How far can you see? Choose something a little bit away—
 maybe a tree or a building. What can you see?
 How much detail can you make out?

Now look through the binoculars or telescope.
 What difference does it make?
 What features can you see that you couldn't see before? Look around
 at some other things. What new aspects do the binoculars let you see?

And then think about a microscope—have you ever looked through one
 to see the intricate detail in some tiny cells? Or the incredible complexity
 of an insect's wing? Just think how much we miss if we only use our eyes.

Read Joel 2:28-29.

The pouring out of God's Spirit enables his people
 to dream dreams, to see visions, to picture new
 possibilities. Like binoculars or a microscope,
 the Spirit brings into focus a new kingdom
 which previously was invisible.

Are you ready for a new way of seeing?
 Are you ready for God to show you his vision for
 your life and this world? Ask God to anoint your dreams,
 to give you a fresh vision of your part in the kingdom.
 Be prepared to see new things, to see the Spirit moving.

Pray.

HOW GOD MET ME

*Thoughts,
feelings,
musings,
dreams,
pictures,
ideas...*

Listen and Learn

The Spirit...moves.
Go to your public library or school library.
Walk the aisles. Flip through the card catalog.
   Visit every floor, every department,
   speaking to as few people as possible.
Watch. Look. Listen.
How much there is to know.
How little of it you've mastered.
Don't despair—you don't need to know everything.
   And if you locked yourself in the library and
   read it all—all the history,
   the novels,
   the poetry,
   the science and technology, everything—
   much of what you learned would be
   out of date long before you seriously
   dented the mountains of material.
What's *really* important to know in order to live your life well?
What insights are essential?
   What truth must you have?
And where do you go for that information?
Here's the good news: You have a tutor.
Read Jesus' words in John 14:25-26.
What is the Holy Spirit teaching you?
   How carefully are you listening?
Pray.

But the Counselor, the Holy Spirit, whom the Father will send in my name, will teach yo... remind you of...

Thoughts,
feelings,
musings,
dreams,
pictures,
ideas...

all things and will
everything I have said to you.

Calming Chaos

The Spirit...moves.
Find a simple puzzle and spread the pieces out on a table or
  on the floor. Stare at them for a moment.
  Notice the disorder.
Think about the world. Where is there disorder?
  Where is there confusion and chaos?
Think about your personal world. Is there confusion there as well?
Begin organizing the pieces and putting the puzzle together.
  As you place each piece,
  think about the picture that is slowly forming.
  Watch as you create order out of chaos.
Read Genesis 1:1-2, 31.
What was the world like in the beginning? What was the Spirit doing?
Our world is often chaotic, but God's Spirit is a force of creation.
The Spirit takes chaos and turns it into beauty,
...takes confusion and turns it into clarity,
...takes disjointed pieces and turns them into a stunning picture.
God's specialty is bringing peaceful creation to chaos.
  He created our world from chaos;
  he made us new creations from the chaos of sin.
What is chaotic in your life? Family? Friends? Future? School?
All of these can cause confusion, stress, and chaos.
  But the Spirit brings creative peace.
  In the middle of the chaos of your life,
  the Spirit hovers,
  just as the Spirit hovered over the formless earth.
Pray that the Spirit would take the chaos and confusion
  of your life and create calm out of chaos.

and it was very

HOW GOD MET ME

Thoughts,
feelings,
musings,
dreams,
pictures,
ideas...

good

Rhythm

The Spirit...moves.

Play a track from your favorite CD, nice and loud.

Sit back and relax. Let the music surround and envelop you.

Tap your feet or your fingers to the rhythm.

Enjoy the way the different instruments blend together
to create a full and funky sound.

Pick out one instrument—maybe the drums, guitar,
or even the singer.

What would happen if that instrument got off tempo?
Imagine the result if it were played too slow...or too
fast...or to its own secret rhythm. (You could try
tapping out these new rhythms with your fingers.)

The beauty and harmony of the music would turn into
a discordant mess. It would be hard to relax and
listen to it. How would it make you feel?

Relax again and enjoy the music as it was meant to be heard.

Read Galatians 5:25.

The Spirit flows through creation, bringing together the
different contributions of God's people to create perfect,
incredible music. All of creation, like the instruments in
your song, is in step...in rhythm...with God's tempo.

Your life is an important part of this beautiful sound.
You help to create a song of beauty and joy. Without
you, it's not quite as rich and moving as it could be.

Are you in step with the Spirit?

Are you playing your part in time? Or are you taking
your cues from somewhere else?

Listen to the music of the Spirit in your heart.

Pray.

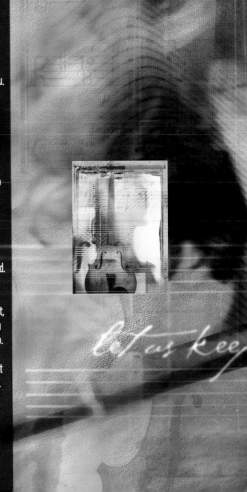

Thoughts,
feelings,
musings,
dreams,
pictures,
ideas...

in step with the Spirit

Feel the Power

The Spirit...moves.
Find a comfortable place to sit—*outdoors*, please.
Now shake up a can of your favorite soft drink.
    Shake it *hard*.
You know what just happened, don't you?
    Inside the can, twelve ounces of highly carbonated,
    highly charged soda is dying to express itself by
    exploding out of the container.
Put your finger on the pull tab. Pause.
What you do next determines what happens to
    the pent-up energy in the can.
    You can pull the tab and free it—
    or do nothing and let it eventually subside.
    If you don't open the can until tomorrow,
    you won't be able to tell how close
    it was to bursting the seams.
It's up to you.
Read 2 Timothy 1:7-8.
The Holy Spirit is in you.
    You weren't given a timid spirit.
    You are filled with God's Spirit of power.
What will you do with that power?
    How will you change the world?
Pray.

BUT A SPIRIT

OF LOVE AND O

S A SPIRIT OF TIMIDITY

Thoughts,
feelings,
musings,
dreams,
pictures,
ideas...

OF POWER,

ELF-DISCIPLINE.